Treasures Of The Heart

Published By

Coral Dawn

By Coral Dawn

This Book Is Dedicated

To My Father

Harry Thomas Evans

With Love

Find out more about Coral Dawn on the following Website or contact information:-

www.coraldawn.com

(The Coral Dawn website is under construction)

www.facebook.com/coral.dawn9026

coral.dawn222@gmail.com

Phone:- 01209 832140   Mobile:- 07876 491354

The Production, Design, Layout and Publishing Facilitated By WebSitesPlus ©2013

www.facebook.com/steve.websitesplus

www.web-sites-plus.com

Email Steve@web-sites-plus.com

Phone:- 01202 873058   Mobile:- 07854 978913

Copyright: Coral Dawn© 2014

All rights reserved. No reproduction, copy or transmission of this publication may be made without written permission. Copyright theft is stealing. No paragraph or picture of this publication may be reproduced, copied or transmitted save with written permission from the author or in accordance with the provisions of the Copyright, Design and Patents Act 1988, or under the terms of any license permitting limited copying issued by the Copyright Licensing Agency, 90 Tottenham Court Rd, London, W1P 9HE, England. Any person who does any unauthorised act in relation to this publication may be liable to criminal prosecution and civil claims for damages. The author has asserted her right to be identified as the author of this work in accordance with the Copyright, Design and Patents Act 1988.

Treasures of the Heart

Acknowledgements

I would like to thank my fiancé and soul-mate Rob for all the caring support and help he has given to me with this book and the joy it has brought to us both. The picture of me on the back of this book was kindly taken by Gayle Force. I would like to thank my cousin Dawn for all the helpful chats and love I have felt concerning my work with this book. Special thanks to my wonderful and special Father for encouraging me so much 'love you Dad', and my three much loved children and all the happy words they have spoken of my work. I would like to mention my two adorable grandchildren that say 'Nana more' xx. A big thank you to my brother Steve for producing and designing this book and all the work he has put into it for me, and I know there's many more to come. Steve was out of the country for a few years previous to this and I missed him very much, but now he is back and we spend lots of time chatting and planning, it's wonderful to have him back in my life. A special thank you to my dearest Mum who passed the gift of poetry to me in the shape of a heart 'love you so much Mum'.

A special thank you to my very close friend Caroline who listened to every poem she could and always with the kindest words of praise.

I would also like to introduce and thank Gayle Force for her wonderful gift of some beautiful pictures that have been added to my books' Treasures of the heart' Special Edition and Treasures of the heart Book 2. I met with Gayle at her home this February and we had such a lovely time together. She listened to some of my poems which she liked very much and one of the poems was named `Dawn is breaking`. Gayle excitedly said she wanted to find a photo that she had taken and would go wonderfully with my poem. She showed me the photo and I asked Gayle if she would mind me adding some of her creative photography to my books. She told me that she would love to be a part of my work and we agreed that we would love to meet again very soon to plan future ideas together. I'm sure that you will be seeing more of Gayle's pictures in my new releases, named 'Whispered Fairy Wishes' all about the fae' folk.

By Coral Dawn

This book will be amusing, healing, colourful, heart-warming and very visual. Also, Rhyming Intentions, a book of rhyming affirmations with the intention to change our lives for the better by reading, saying, thinking, feeling and believing what we want to happen in our lives.

Gayle's Story

When I first met Coral it was a cold and blustery February day. We hurried inside to begin our time together. I had already learned that Coral was a talented poet. Settling in with a cup of china tea, Coral began to choose and read some of her work to me.

I sat and listened, closed my eyes, and as the poem unraveled, it was about a tree in Respryn, a place I know well, and I was gone. It was very moving, and I found myself with a tear in my eye. Like Coral I love trees and being amongst the wonders of Mother Nature. It will be a favorite of mine and most likely yours too. Other poems followed on, each with its own individual delight. Each time, I could picture myself within the writings, and within the place that Coral had written about. These writings had a great familiarity to them.

Coral is a talented, spiritual writer that creates a feeling within you. Almost meditative, with a fleeting touch of magic. In between these pages of moving work, Coral invited me to bring her poetry even more alive with some of my creative photography that I have collected over many years for such an occasion. I am delighted to be a part of this wonderful book and to be able to bring an atmospheric addition to it too. I am even more delighted to have met Coral.

Now a little bit about myself. I am famous for my work as a healer/medium/clairvoyant and I am known internationally. I have featured on BBC T.V and radio as well as many others. I also write articles and columns for magazines. I begun photography from around the age of fourteen. It has been

Treasures of the Heart

a part of my artistic and creative expression. As well as personal photo shoots I also find my work lends itself to commercial work too. My hope is that you will enjoy the photos that the author of this book and I have chosen to enhance each poems story, and I hope that they may be inspiring as well as healing, just as I feel Corals poems are very healing.

With Love and Light Energies from Gayle Force, Cornish Healer/ Medium/ Writer.

By Coral Dawn
<u>Introduction</u>

When I was a little girl there were two things that I loved to do. I loved to sing and to write. My first teacher at my school in Walthamstow, East London, told me that I was very good at English and poetry. My mother always wrote poems in Christmas and birthday cards and that continued until she passed away seventeen years ago. I wrote lots of short stories as a little girl, and one in particular, my special cousin Dawn can still remember named 'Princess Daisy'.

When my Mother passed, the tradition of writing our poetry in cards unfortunately seemed to dwindle away. Then about three years ago I was Diagnosed with a tumour in my left lung and decided to try to heal it myself. So, I visited many places in Cornwall where I now live. Saint Neot was one of the lovely places that I made a visit to and one of the magical things about this very special, beautiful and peaceful place is its sacred Holy Well. I left blessings of herbs, flowers and crystals and I prayed. I also visualised my lungs healthy and said many healing affirmations (which will be included in another book I have in the pipe-line called "Rhyming Intentions" aimed to help toward good health and well-being). I was with my special partner Rob when he said he would go for a little walk up the woodland track, so I sat on the grass above the well under the tree when I sensed sheer peace and words coming to me. I always carry a little note pad in my bag and began to write.

Treasures of the Heart

Poetry was just flowing; I wrote two poems in that time and they are included in this book. I continued to visit sacred places to pray and give blessings where I met some lovely people and wrote many more beautiful poems. I also visited some churches to be close to God and pray.

After having several tests and doing lots of healing I had another follow-up x-ray and my consultant said "It seems to have vanished, it is just showing pneumonia". As I have great faith and belief, I wasn't shocked or surprised, just very thankful.

God has always played a big part in my life. I have always spoken to him and asked him to help me and others and always said "thank you" sending healing to the Universe and giving God my love.

I have always been very sensitive towards life itself in every way and wouldn't harm anything. My motto being, if they are here on this planet earth, God has put them here for a reason. So if a fly would be drowning in a puddle or a worm going dry in the sun, I will always save them.

I have always seen and heard spirits and have telepathically spoken to wild life and nature. One of my first experiences with spirit was when I was very young and always slept in my Mother's bed as my Father always worked nights and I didn't like being on my own.

I remember waking from my sleep and laying on my side facing away from my Mother. I saw a young lady kneeling by my side of the bed and on the floor, she was staring at me. She had long dark hair and piercing eyes, and she was there for a long time. I tried to wake my Mother to tell her but she didn't look or believe me, she was not properly awake and she thought I was dreaming thought this was normal though and spoke to my cousin Dawn about it. I asked her if she sees or hears things and she said "no". My Grandmother on my Mother's side always saw fairies at the bottom of her garden and my Mother didn't believe that either, she would say 'she's gone mad'. My spiritual path slowed down when my three beautiful and dearly loved children were

By Coral Dawn

growing up, but when my mother passed away, that all changed and I needed answers. My mother was my best friend and I miss her so much. I talk to her and see her in the spirit world but I would love a big Mummy hug.

My two gorgeous grandchildren are four and five years old and they both love to hear my poetry. They may not understand it completely, but they feel and enjoy the way that I tell it to them. I love them dearly. My Father passed away just over a year ago and in the process of publishing this book. Words cannot express how much I miss him. He was a very special man; He had a heart of gold and would do or help anyone if he could. He taught me how to be who I am and how important it is to care for others and tend Gods' nature. He had so much faith and love for me and told me many times to show someone my work and to get it printed in books, or newspaper, or something. 'Just get it out there'

So here I am.......

Treasures of the Heart

Index

5.	....	Acknowledgements
8.	....	Introduction
14.	....	The Calling Skies
16.	....	Bodmin Moor
18.	....	Amongst The Field Of Daffodils
20.	....	Generosity
22.	....	Autumn Leaves
24.	....	The Bird
26.	....	The Icy lake.
28.	....	Dawn Is Breaking
30.	....	Beauty
32.	....	Soft Sensations.
34.	....	The Magic Tree
36.	....	Pain
38.	....	Wise Woman
40.	....	The Ghost in the lake
42.	....	Spring
44.	....	The Garden Of Words
46.	....	The Waterfall Of Life
48.	....	The Hedgerows Of My Mind
50.	....	The Moon That's Me
52.	....	Success
54.	....	Water
56.	....	Precious Moments
58.	....	The Spirit Of The Wishing Star
60.	....	Sunshine Paradise
62.	....	The Swan

By Coral Dawn

64.	....	The Woodland
66.	....	The Breathing Waters
68.	....	Healing
70.	....	The Cotton Cloud
72.	....	Purple Mist
74.	....	My Home Inside The Wishing Well
76.	....	Field Of Promise
78.	....	Butterflies
80.	....	The Healer
82.	....	Forgiveness
84.	....	Scarlet Sky
86.	....	Autumn
88.	....	Colours Of Love
90.	....	My Home
92.	....	Love Is A Balanced Ocean
94.	....	The Friend That Lives Inside Me
96.	....	The Tiny Waterfall
98.	....	The Field Of Sunflowers
100.	....	The Box At The Bottom Of The Stream
102.	....	Thank You
104.	....	The Hawk
106.	....	Thinking Of Our Love
108.	....	The Robin
110.	....	Angels
112.	....	Colour
114.	....	Gratitude
116.	....	Golden Sand

Treasures of the Heart

118. ....Hedgerows
120. ....Live The Joy In Everything
122. ....The Man That Sells Wood
126. ....Her Calling
127. ....I Heard A Silent Lullaby
128. ....The Tree That Talks To Me
130. ....The Storm
132. ....Waves Of Song
134. ....The Shop
136. ....The Ghost Within My Mind
138. ....The Old Bench Of Wishes
140. ....Wind
142. ....The Summerhouse
144. ....Nature
146. ....Mallard
148. ....The Sky
150. ....Where I Go To Be With You
152. ....Treasures Of The Heart
154. .... Contribution
155. .... Family and friends that helped

By Coral Dawn

The Calling Skies

Blue as forget-me-nots, looking at me
Blue as the ocean when sun greets the sea
Feathery splashes of warm summer days
Sun's dazzling patterns of yellowing rays
A rainbow of colour that bows to the sea
Its shimmering smile as it beckons to me
Fluffy pearl cushions of white softened clouds
With mottled-blessed secrets, caressing in crowds
Layers of amber that blaze through the sun
Reminding each cloud with its face in each one
Warm burning sky showing scarlet-red lust
An opulent sphere of a flaming-gold rust
Lavender clouds through a blanket of mist
The hot setting sun that the dusk has just kissed
The silvery moon that suspends in mid-air
The stars of our wishes to answer each prayer
Dawn that awakens its life through the trees
Like mystical beings that dance in the breeze
The moon is its heart and the sun is its breath
The stars are the angels we thank and we bless

Treasures of the Heart

By Coral Dawn

Bodmin Moor

A feeling of peace, of infinite life and beauty beyond compare
Grasses swaying gracefully with elegance they share
Holiness and sacredness and energy within
Clover dancing merrily that brush against your skin
Streams go winding through the green as ripples flow in time
With sun that's looking down with love and smiling as he shines
Trees are blessed with posies to say thank you for this place
Life is beating naturally through silent time and space
Buds are opening, lives emerging, hearing all Gods' words
Trees emitting oxygen and holding nests for birds
The beauty of the moors assures us peace with God above
His special place is filled with grace and pure, eternal love

Treasures of the Heart

By Coral Dawn

Amongst The Field Of Daffodils

Amongst the field of daffodils a secret swing exists

Its seat is wooded sable which swings in a silver mist

Ivy's wound around the ropes that hold it 'bov the ground

With grasses swaying, reaching high and daisies all around

The swing has secret powers that will help the folk in need

So when they sit upon the seat their hopes and dreams succeed

Mist will lift, sun will shine, in rays of flaming gold

The daffodils will emanate their scent for hearts to hold

As it swings its hopeful guests they'll hear an angel's song

The lyrics soft and beautiful with notes that flow along

"Trust in love" the voice will tell, "your dreams will then come true"

"Always act through happiness in everything you do"

The swing will then sit silently in hazy summer heat

Waiting for the next time, that a guest sits 'pon the seat

Treasures of the Heart

By Coral Dawn

Generosity

When you give deep from your heart, the gift will not be missed
Kindness from your caring heart's rewarded with a kiss
If you act with graciousness or use it for another
It is an act of Gods' pure love to bring our hearts together
So give a gift, help someone, or grant a special deed
For when we add these to our lives they help us to succeed
It's Gods' pure plan of only love to guide our special lives
We must all come together which will help us grow and thrive
So, when your help is needed and you act and do your part
Angel's will be watching to reward your special heart

Treasures of the Heart

By Coral Dawn

Autumn Leaves

As the leaves fall from the trees they dance about the sky
They softly float in autumn breeze, and use the wind to fly
Crispy leaves fall down in time and find a place to settle
They blow within the softened air, as tender as a petal
Crimson-plum that's edged with gold, a fragrant earthy scent
Warming sunlight shining down reflecting sweet intent
Golden wafers whisk and dance upon the woodland track
They blend together 'neath a tree in golden, fibrous stacks
They drink the stream to join as one and flow in perfect time
Rejoicing natures' rippling life as tints of water shine
They meet a bird and stroke his wings in mid-air joyous flight
They feel the sunshine in the sky and tender clouds of white
They find their way to fields of green to warm the grass from frost
They gently fill their chosen place with leaves of amber gloss
The wind blows freely through the trees
As leaves fly from their homes
They fall like rain and fill the sky with orange, coppered tones
As nature works its Godly plan to strive for life and birth
The autumn season starts its change with honour, love and mirth

Treasures of the Heart

By Coral Dawn

The Bird

Freely flowing through the sky of fluffy cotton clouds
Mottled aqua peeping through its ambience endowed
She opens up and spreads her wings, engaging with the air
The sun gleams rays of golden light to touch her in mid-air
She waves her graceful feather wings to find her heart of song
She calls the power of her dreams to drive her will along
She moves her head with tender grace through softened pearly sky
She strokes against the sunshine heat and soars her spirit high
She fills herself with pure delight, embracing all she is
Ecstasy and happiness is all she wants to give
She senses love within her soul to spread her grace through earth
Her source of drive, her natural life, and purpose of her birth
She meets her mate and gifts her heart inside his very soul
They fly as one, of mirrored love, to follow natures' role

Treasures of the Heart

By Coral Dawn

The Icy Lake

It's very cold deep down inside the very ice lake
As silence tries to holds me down, my terror starts to wake
It fills me up with darkness and the greying winter skies
It tries to soothe my frozen heart by flowing to my cries
It touches me as cold as ice and whispers in my ear
It floods down deep within my mind to things I always fear
The crown of ice that sits upon the frozen icy lake
Melts down to form some cracks
Before my saddened heart will break
I see the light above me like some glints of hope in sight
The rain falls down upon me like the tears of darkened night
Lurking down below me is the past of things before
Tangled words of demons, when my doubts show up once more
Please let me be happy in this cold and icy lake
Please heat up my broken dreams that will my heart to wake

Treasures of the Heart

By Coral Dawn

Dawn Is Breaking

Sunshine rising 'bove the cliffs, like walls of flaming fire
Reflecting 'pon the ocean like a glowing orange spire
Lighting up the morning sky like amber through a flame
With coral mist just floating by, like ghosts across the plain
High up in the dawning sky, the clouds blush fuchsia pink
They lie on beds of luscious gold where colours merge and link
Meeting grass that catches light, reflecting golden-green
Shining on a glassy lake like visions of a dream
Peeping 'bove the ocean wall, an arc of gleaming light
Looking through the hazy sky of mystic pearly white
Tiers of cloud-break in the sky with mountains in between
Mirroring fluorescent hints of rays across a stream
Directing lights to heaven like hot torches through the sun
Announcing to the planet that the day has just begun
Rising up above the clouds, a round sulphurous fire
Dawn awakes another day to cherish and admire

Treasures of the Heart

By Coral Dawn

<u>Beauty</u>

Children's faces full of love and smiling with delight
Adult birds that feed their young, a precious, happy sight
Trees that blow in autumn wind and glow like bronzing fire
A ballerina on her toes to watch her and admire
A horse that births her foal and tends the suckling of her young
A bird so full of happiness while singing natures' song
A view upon the cliff-tops of the seas' raw, natural state
A swan that paddles silent streams and snuggles with his mate
Flowers in their splendour, like a shock of scented wonder
Apples falling from the trees and light-days that grows longer
All these things are beautiful and gifts we have to hold
The warmth of summer sunshine and the icicles so cold
If we feel the beauty and can hold it in our hearts
We'll see that love has been with us right from the very start

Treasures of the Heart

By Coral Dawn

Soft Sensations

Water flowing down the stream and softly passing by
Birds that flock together while they play high in the sky
Sun that shines upon me as it settles on my face
Sand that blows through summer breeze with elegance and grace

Soft grass brushing on my toes and looking to the light
The waxing moon in starry sky, a silver of the night
Petals floating tenderly in airy soft perfume
Grains of sand adjoining, to reflect a desert dune

Fruits that ripen in the sun then drop down from their trees
Cherry blossoms swaying showing red tints through their leaves
Oceans calm as silence as they meet the salty shore
Snowflakes soft and fluffy as their ice begins to thaw

Water lilies floating by and filling soft the lake
Dew drops on the ivy that fall down before they wake
Hazy sun caressing me on cliff tops by the sea
Soft sensations everywhere, they're meant for you and me

Treasures of the Heart

By Coral Dawn

The Magic Tree

Standing proud, a centrepiece of magical delight
Leaves of reddened-amber held on arms of lightened night
Pointed leaves like glossy stars and ambience that glows
A wooded body strong and bold with hints of sunshine gold
Dancing on her grassy home she sways the breeze of earth
Her roots grow deep and plentiful as life obeys her birth
She breathes the air in thankful time and basks beneath the sun
She waits in silent motion for the quenching rain to come
Then showers rain upon her like a spray of fountain mist
A cooling crystal flurry of the things her heart has wished
When the sun is setting she awaits to greet the moon
She reaches to the sky with branchy arms of leafy bloom
He shows his face upon her as she shines with silvered sheen
She gives her wishes to the moon of every hopeful thing
She gives her thanks and deepest love below the midnight glory
She ends her night with many prayers of every healing story

Treasures of the Heart

By Coral Dawn

Pain

Pain is something we create when life is upside down

A break up with a loved one or a friend gives us a frown

It doesn't matter big or small the problem that you get

Perhaps a meeting you can't make that you have promptly set

Remember as the problem niggles down inside your mind

It travels round your body making illness of all kinds

So keep your feelings healthy, and divinely full of love

The reality will be pain-free, as pure as Heaven above

Treasures of the Heart

By Coral Dawn

Wise Woman

She tends her garden full of herbs

She fills her mind with healing words

Her inner-knowing shines to see

She sits beneath her willow tree

She knows the wisdom that trees behold

Elixirs and potions she doth enfold

She heals the earth on everyday

She tends nature in every way

Her familiar the cat is wise and healing

It's faithful and senses her every feeling

The wise-woman's home is her creation

With trinkets and chimes of decoration

Herbs drying from her windows and ceilings

She adds them to tinctures especially for healing

Her hands are a comfort and radiate heat

Her presence is soothing, her spirit is sweet

She speaks to the souls of life times that pass

She tells folk their fortune, her powers are vast

This is her true essence since all life began

To move her toward Gods' most sanctified plan

She fills every life with the beauty of love

And heals those in need through our dear Lord above

Treasures of the Heart

By Coral Dawn

The Ghost In The Lake

Lurking 'bove the midnight lake a ghostly fog exists
He creeps about so silently, his presence might be missed
He brushes 'pon the lily leaves and sweeps across the banks
His mist of silver chiffon quenches thirst of trees with thanks
He sees himself inside the lake as sun begins to rise
He dances changing all his shapes, and reaches far and wide
Sunshine lights his murky mist with tones of gold and red
He floats along the glassy lake to where his mind is led
He swirls around the edging plants like notions of a dream
He leaves his patterns in the mist of all forgotten things
Dew drops wave their shiny lives to beckon him adieu
Whilst ghostly haze enchants the lake rejoicing all that's new

Treasures of the Heart

By Coral Dawn

<u>Spring</u>

Spring buds from its chilly sleep of restful winter days
It stretches out and reaches through a sunlit silvery-haze
Crocus peep as snow-drops yawn, and bow to say goodbye
While dancing 'neath the whispering wind of periwinkle sky
Trees bear forth their new-green shoots while bathing in the sun
And birds sing songs of love and mirth for each and every one
The warming sun sends hints of light upon the buds of spring
As new birth gift their posies that this joyous season brings
Florets white with cherry-pink and glossy emerald leaves
Creatures bathe in spring perfume and spicy woodland breeze
Windflowers smile 'neath sunshine light beside the babbling stream
Whilst bloodroot pops its head up high of petalled silky cream
Grasses grow so tall and proud and blend with minted herbs
Trees with buds of berried fruit holds nests for thankful birds
Along the bronzing woodland-track the dazzling moss pink crawls
Creatures wake up all around to hear the season call
Winter brings us endings, but it's only for a while
For when the spring comes once again it brings our hearts to smile

Treasures of the Heart

By Coral Dawn

The Garden Of Words

A place called Nancegollan is where this garden grows
Everything is cared through love, which every flower shows
Roses bear soft faces as they share their thanks with smiles
With scent from soothing lavender that spreads for miles and miles
Buttercups that open up to drink the summer sun
Whilst sharing all their happiness of golden days to come
Trailing spring lobelia that fall out from their tubs
Stretching out with eagerness to meet the waiting shrubs
A bird house in the centre that is made from cedar wood
With twisted hazel round the base and grasses 'cross the hood
An old worn chair of sable wood is where the lady sits
Each side upon her special chair are daisies in the slits
She talks to all her flowers and she sings to all her trees
Blossoms gift their love to her while swaying in the breeze
The wall along the garden fence meets pretty golden fields
It's where her many bird friends sit with songs she always feels
She plants her seeds whilst speaking grace to all their special lives
They thank her with their fondest love that shows within her eyes
Her cat looks up toward her face to thank of joy at last
The lady hears her calling words and tends to all they ask
It is the place she feels at home and close to God above
She tends her garden every day with promise of her love
Her mother passed this to her, of the way a garden feels
To sit amongst the natural life can soothe the heart to heal

Treasures of the Heart

By Coral Dawn

The Waterfall Of Life

I flow down over river banks like waves of pouring rain
Breathing life and energy that pulses through each vein
Hazy mist engulfs me as it hovers 'pon my sheen
Dawn awakes with morning sun that brightens every dream
I live beneath the turquoise sky, adorned with angel's words
Basking in the vision of the suns' glint catching birds
I reach out far to touch them with a spray of bubbly mist
I calmly ripple meekly meeting silence with a kiss
The light pours down upon me showing sunlight through the trees
Fountains filter through me like a tempest in a breeze
Grasses dance upon the banks whilst looking to the light
With scattered flowering buttercups that fill my heart so bright
Pebbled stones go bobbing past to find where they belong
Brushing 'gainst each other and in time with nature's song
As I flow through time and space and day becomes the night
My spirit guides my waterfall to live through healing light

Treasures of the Heart

By Coral Dawn

The Hedgerows Of My Mind

Looking through the twisted vines that sit inside my mind
Hoping that the sun shines light through hopes for me to find
Many times my dreams have overtaken all my fears
Watching as the hedgerow shows me hope through all the years

Sitting on a wall and glancing up toward the trees
Colours peeping through them telling stories of my dreams
Noticing the breeze that catches birds up in the sky
Pecking at the hedgerows of my mind as they go by

Swaying leaves through misty sky, calms whispers in my mind
The scarlet fire of setting sun burns imprints that I find
I will the sun to smile on me to warm my troubled mind
The hedgerows of my heart will help me leave the past behind

Lying on the grass and letting worries drift away
Thinking 'bout the happy times and memories of each day
Looking at the canopy as hedges meet as one
Dreaming that one day my time for happiness will come

Treasures of the Heart

By Coral Dawn

The Moon That's Me

In a ball of spangled light
My flowing hair shines through the night
Existing in my lunar sphere
My silver sheen is pure and clear
Dancing with my starry friends
Their jewels gleam as light extends
I drink the rain to cleanse my soul
To heal with light, my chosen goal
I look upon the earth with love
Creating from the world above
I breathe the sky and wash with rain
I sleep when dawn will rise again
I bless the sun of golden light
Of flaming passion shining bright
His confidence shines out to see
I answer when he calls to me
I rest above the tallest trees
The elements tend all my needs
I live and thrive in misty bliss
My thoughts are true of all I wish
I catch your thoughts in silver haze
My aura shows them through your days
Always word your wishes well
Your stories truth is what I tell

Treasures of the Heart

By Coral Dawn

Success

When you strive towards your goal
It makes you feel alive and whole
Strive towards your hearts desire
For what you yearn will then transpire
Your faith will make your dreams come true
Giving joy in all you do
Focus on the goal you need
And then in sequence plant your seed
Feel it happen, watch it grow
Watch your triumph spread and glow
Whatever your goal it can be done
It builds and grows for everyone
Whatever we feel within our minds
Is what our mirrored world will find
So keep your vision clear and clean
And then create your special dream

Treasures of the Heart

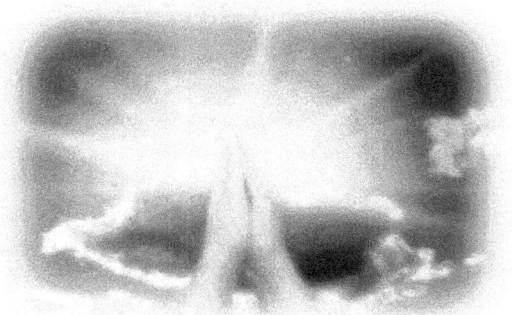

By Coral Dawn

Water

The dew of early morning and the stream that flows along
The waves that roll and make a splash and sing their cooling song
The water breaking on the shore as rain drops gently fall
The storm that hits the window-pane when autumn makes its call
Tear drops when we cry of news that's either good or bad
A cool drink from a wishing well to show the good we have
The snowflakes that form pictures on a very icy day
The vast breath-taking wonder of a rugged seashore bay
A glassy lake of sea-through sheen displaying beams of sun
With tiny sprays of fizzy mist and warmer days to come
Dew-drops in the morning clearly sparkling bright like pearls
The saltiness of Ocean Sea that lives inside its shell
Flakes of icy falling snow that chills the silver sky
A graceful spirit of the lake that splays her wings to fly
Droplets seeping into earth to quench the thirsty trees
The flossy-white of snow drops that display a winter freeze
We give our thanks as we prepare to sing our song of prayer
For all the gifts that fill our lives and everything we share

Treasures of the Heart

By Coral Dawn

Precious Moments

Waltzing round the woodland trees, chasing in the summer breeze
Touching daises with our toes, smiles of laughter that we show
Rolling down the grassy hill, glancing at the turning mill
Sun that shines upon the stream, wonder of each special dream
Precious moments waltzing by, memories of the joy I cry
Happy times spent by the sea, children smiling up at me
Day-dreams when I kiss their cheeks
To give them all the love they seek
Happy moments dancing through
Blessing smiles through morning dew
Children sitting in their swings, tender times and all they bring
Climbing up the teasing trees, always quick to love and please
A new generation; sparkling eyes, hopes of triumph, happy cries
Special days of singing games, skipping through the pouring rain
Balloons of life and tender times
Stories, games and nursery rhymes
Birthday cake and candled light, future hope of lives so bright
Special love for everyone, with so much more that's yet to come
Their spirits fill me up with pride, happy when there by my side
I thank the Lord that I am blessed with children full of happiness

Treasures of the Heart

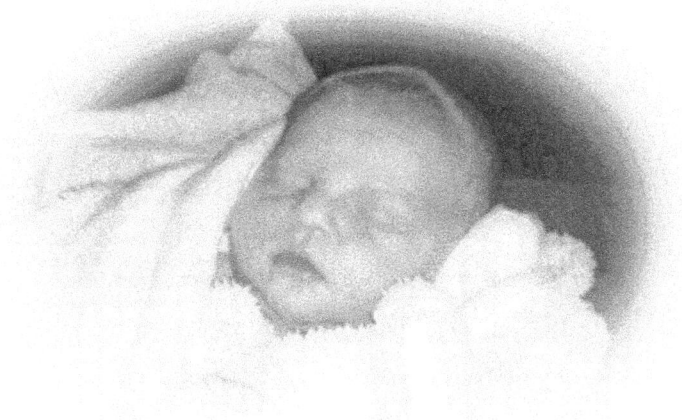

By Coral Dawn

The Spirit Of The Wishing Star

My face is glowing silver and my limbs are pointing peaks
I reach to touch the heavens as I ask for all you seek
My breath is airy moonshine that reflects your every need
I fill the sky with visions of your ever-growing dreams
My spirit dances 'pon the clouds as shining hopes to grow
I glisten to an angel's call that tells me all I know
My life reflects on rippled lakes that drink my healing light
I'm lucent and entrancing; I'm a beacon of the night
My purpose and my pathway is to shine with love to see
To bring my callers' dreams alive and set their spirits free
I will you to look up at me and fill your life with love
And as you do I'll light your heart while shining from above

Treasures of the Heart

By Coral Dawn

Sunshine Paradise

Sunshine peeping silently above a wall of mist
A picture landscape paradise of cloudy mountain bliss
Rays of sunshine lighting clouds that fill the hazy sky
Sending sparks of flaming-gold that glisten as they fly
Shapely clouds appear in peaks, like cliffs of early June
As sunshine catches silvered light to greet the waxing moon
Rays of sun hit turquoise sky that blend a greenish-pink
The brightness of the lightened hues flash past before they link
Looking like a flower shooting petals into space
Reaching to the heavens, meeting earth without a trace
Like a ball of cosmic mist that spirals from its core
Lighting sea that rolls along like jewels on the shore
As the rays stretch openly to warm the tips of trees
It glides along the branches as it merges with their leaves
Strong and bold with confidence of all it can achieve
Giving gifts of lightened joy to every life in need

Treasures of the Heart

By Coral Dawn

The Swan

Pure as bliss, exquisite grace, a softened kiss of love
In the lake her feathered silk is blessed by God above
Wading waters forest green she searches for her reason
Divinely gliding, gaily admiring, the newness of the season
She splashes in the ripples as she bathes herself in beauty
She shakes her softness warmly as she longs to find her duty
She teases fish and dips her beak, she flaps her mighty wings
She takes her flight in natures' sky and feels her sadness sing
She stands beneath a willow tree and finds her life-long mate
She lays her neck embracing his; they snuggle and elate
They spend their days rejoicing life and living joy together
They warm their eggs of bonding love they know will last forever
Their cygnets hatch and peep at life as sun sends beams of light
Their parents joined together and rejoicing at their sight
They swim the lake of hope and mirth with hearts of promised kisses
As long as God knows what we yearn, he answers all our wishes

Treasures of the Heart

By Coral Dawn

The Woodland

At the gold of midday sun the cuckoo flower sways its leaves
A squirrel grabs his acorns from the oak tree as he weaves
The fox-glove shows its dome-shaped cups of pinking, purple bells
The jay-bird screams behind the hedge
As new morn wakes and tells
The yew-trees branches curve and stretch to find some earth to root
As buttercups of sunshine give their birth to summer shoots
A chaffinch sings his loudest song and eats his chickweed meal
The twisted ivy covers ground, as sky birds start to squeal
Hedging mustard's pepper-face shines through with lemon beauty
As spiderwort, the gift of earth, rejoices in her duty
Rabbits with their tender young sniff air and nibble grass
A butterfly of olive-green sends love as she flies past
The fever-few of daises bear their scented, pungent smell
The blackberry lily of iris give us blooms that stories tell
The gold-crest scuffles through the trees
And sings his high-pitched song
Sparrows' chitter-chatter as they move the air along
The silver birch, of graceful light, gives life of heart-shaped leaves
Her seeds that fly by through the wind, give love to all in need
A little babbling woodland brook reflect the glints of sun
The eye-bright growing gracefully will nourish everyone
Ginger, of the forest, shows her flowers 'neath her leaves

Treasures of the Heart

Marsh-Marigold, spring glory, gives her nectar to the bees
Rattle-weed shows candled blooms to light the woodland way
A place of God and love intent in every special day
When we see this earthly place of wondrous sheer delight
We give our thanks and send our love and fill it up light

By Coral Dawn

The Breathing Waters

Rolling in time like the beat of a drum

Ripples of life, with a breath in each one

Patches of emerald through turquoise and green

With light reaching out through a translucent sheen

Splashes of froth as the waves reached the shore

Then water touched earth as the clear-droplets poured

The sea changed its colours like shapes in a maze

The sun shone its light through a gold misty-haze

Crashing on rocks while declaring its power

Then sun caught a spray through a transparent shower

Its calmness to change in its every clear motion

As peace and pure silence empowered the ocean

Taking commands from a change in the sky

With vast intense surges and waves that reached high

Water met air and the warm fiery sun

Fusing with earth and embracing each one

Filling the breeze as it chattered its song

Clapping together and chasing along

Its spirit alive as it breathed in content

And waters secreting their heavenly-scent

Treasures of the Heart

By Coral Dawn

Healing

We ask for healing in our desperate pain
Why does it feel like a hurricane?
It blows and it whirls with anger and fear
And all is but so very clear
We create the opposite of our very core
And forget to open the Holy door
The place that guides our very soul
And answers to our every goal
So as we turn our chosen key
Or lightened path we choose to see
Remember to open the Holy door
To find the things you're searching for

Treasures of the Heart

By Coral Dawn

The Cotton Cloud

Peeping 'bove a veil of cloud the sun shines bright as gold
Orange flames of golden light our thankful hearts can hold
Warming through the clear blue sky a path to show the way
With lines of rays that travelled through like paths of yesterday
Ignited like a torch of flames and heating all the land
The beams of sun passed through the trees reflecting where I stand
Shades of pink and purple mist that edged the dappled sky
Glints that shone upon the clouds that meld as they moved by
Honeyed sprays of sunlit joy that journeyed to my heart
With luscious rays of ruby red each side the sunlight starts
Hazy landscapes we can build with pictures in our dreams
Like stacks of coloured pyramids with glory that they bring
Sunlight glowing through the clouds like beacons guide the way
That open like a flower on a warming summers' day

Treasures of the Heart

By Coral Dawn

Purple Mist

I swirl around the rocks and trees
I blend within the warming breeze
Lavender dust with silver-blue
Moody calm of misty hue
With hazy lust I fill the skies
I drink the beauty of disguise
I skim and touch the earthly ground
Like softened feathers' airy sound
A sandy spray of lilac dreams
With scattered clouds and painted scenes
My flowing legs reach down through earth
To meet the roots that gave their birth
My giving arms touch soft the trees
They brush against the rippled seas
My hair falls over river banks
I kiss his flow to give my thanks
A reddish blend; a mist of time
Existing through a love divine
Violet love and purple mist
See through rain of dawn's first kiss
Peace and bliss is what I bring
To live the joy in everything

Treasures of the Heart

By Coral Dawn

My Home Inside The Wishing Well

Along a woodland track and way yonder near a dell
I live my life of wonder down inside a wishing well
My water of emotions ripple soft in perfect time
Callers with their wisely words will wish in sacred rhyme
My body's made with crimson brick and Cornish healing stone
They hold my heart of tenderness within my wishing home
A twisted rope holds tight my bale of all the askers' gifts
It swings just like a pendulum that answers every wish
The sun looks down upon me as it lights up every dream
With golden coins reflecting brightened glints on everything
The grasses dance before me as they kiss the summer breeze
I'm shaded from the heated days by weeping willow trees
The birds sit down upon me as they bless me with their song
The daisies bob through silent wind of days that flow along
I'm peaceful and inviting to the folk that visit me
I do my work of wishes as I shine with love to see

Treasures of the Heart

By Coral Dawn

Field Of Promise

Grasses swaying in the breeze, dancing with the willow trees

Poppies smiling to the sun, dreamy petals on each one

A butterfly she hovers down, with silver wings and golden crown

The swaying grass touch soft her wing,

As natures' gold-crests start to sing

The sun pours light upon the field, a glowing triumph is revealed

Daises gift their lives of white, with mustard centres soft and bright

They move in time with grassy leaves

And welcome busy bumble bees

Buttercups of summer bells, thanking sun with scented smells

The scratchy sounds of touching stems

The shyness of the secret wren

He sneaks upon the rowan tree, and sings his song of joy with glee

The rushes blow their feather-heads

Beneath the sky of shepherd red

A field of promise and natural pleasure

To freely bless with love forever

Treasures of the Heart

By Coral Dawn

Butterflies

Elegantly dancing, magically entrancing, upon a petalled rose
Flapping breeze, feeling leaves, a dainty, graceful show
Saffron gold and leafy green, her wings of gleaming sheen
As buttercups through sunshine-rays pour light upon the stream
She settles on some daises with their orange-mustard smiles
Embracing silky petals as she hovers for a while
She touches soft the summer wind of pale-blue pictured sky
She strokes the silky clouds of white and soars herself so high
She thanks this wondrous summer day of blooming floral bliss
She smells the scented summer breeze and gifts a tansy kiss
Softly sweet her spiral grace of lustrous shiny gold
She carries gifts of tender love her gentle spirit holds
She circles with the damsel flies around their hawthorn tree
She fans her luscious splendour for the whole wide-world to see
She knows of all her beauty that she savours from within
She flits her wings of graceful love to special woodland kin

Treasures of the Heart

By Coral Dawn

The Healer

She is gifted with magic from lifetimes before
A healer to some but to others much more
She knows every answer, her knowledge is wise
She makes all her choices through merciful eyes
She teaches clear thinking and focussed intention
Her mind of believing becomes her creation
Her powers of magic and work with the moon -
Are her greatest of pleasures to which she's attuned
She works with her instinct and heals through her wisdom
She honours the moon and its accurate rhythm
She cares for the planet with healing and herbs
She blesses all nature with jubilant words
She sees passers' spirits with stories to tell
She senses their souls and the places they dwell
She cares for the trees and tends to the earth
She endearingly nurtures each special new birth
She councils the sadness and heals others sorrow
She comforts their tears and the answers they borrow
Her promise is love that she sees through her eyes
While journeying on in her knowing disguise

Treasures of the Heart

By Coral Dawn

Forgiveness

When we hold on tight to feelings of pain

Unhappiness niggles again and again

When we forgive and release there is peace inside

There's an infinite presence, our eternal guide

If we let go of torment or worrying feelings

Then our body and mind will begin with its healing

It's how our lives are meant to be

Filled with love for all to see

For when we release our sadness and sorrow

There will always be a joyous tomorrow

Treasures of the Heart

By Coral Dawn

Scarlet Sky

I drove on by the scarlet sky one day the month of June
The sun was setting burnish-red to meet the crescent moon
I parked the car up on a cliff as light began to wane
The scarlet sky reflected down for night to show again
I stayed a while to watch the view of dreamy scarlet sky
It turned a kinda crimson-gold as daylight passed on by
I drove back home to get some rest one night that month of June
I looked way up through scarlet sky and saw the silver moon
I laid my head upon my bed and closed my eyes up tight
I dreamt that dreamy scarlet sky was warmly glowing bright
It wrapped itself around me like a cloak of cloudy mist
It showed me signs that all my dreams will grant me all I wish

Treasures of the Heart

By Coral Dawn

Autumn

The magical season of autumn is a lovely sight to see
The fading leaves of tawny, green fall down from every tree
Rustic colours peep at us surrounding woodland banks
The willow drops its coppered leaves whilst giving humble thanks
Golden sunlight shining down reflects its glints of flame
The oak tree bears its acorns through a mist of chiffon rain
The rowan carries berries of a crimson, scarlet blush
Falling leaves take on their place in cool winds sweeping gusts
The catkins of the silver birch gift glowing honey hues
The sky shows through the autumn trees with periwinkle blue
The leaves roll 'bout and tumble on the dusty woodland track
With sounds of scratchy touches as they gather in a stack
A stream of glinted ripples rush on past a scented splendour
With heather sprays of violet-pink that sway so soft and tender
Robins find a crevice making home inside a tree
Displaying rose-red feathers for their kin and all to see
The wind goes whirling through the trees
And whispers earthly stories
As seasons change and gift our lives with wondrous autumn glory

Treasures of the Heart

By Coral Dawn

Colours of Love

Every time you're near me love bright rainbows fill my mind
You touch my lips and hold me close, our happiness combined
Birds sing songs as flowers sway and magic fills inside
Forever love, both you and me, together hearts applied

Everything's complete dear, when your love is soft and near
I feel so full of your embrace my life becomes so clear
As long as you are happy, then my sun will always shine
The sea will sparkle jewelled love with your strong hand in mine

Your eyes fill me with passion; I can see inside your soul
I kiss your breath and bathe in love, connection makes us whole
I see your smile inside me as it whispers to my heart
I see your sense of humour and that grin right from the start

It fills me up with colours and the stars of midnight sky
Your soft side and your tender ways that bring my heart to cry
Your happiness is mine dear, like the golden-amber sun
Your dreams and goals are special love, I honour every one

As long as you are happy, and you find your love in me
We'll flow in time together love, the way it's meant to be
We'll flow in time together love, with you dear holding me

Treasures of the Heart

By Coral Dawn

My Home

My home is brimming with angel's voices
With decorations of loving choices
Crystals of plenty with magical meanings
Herb-sprinkled posies with heart-blessed feelings
Rainbows of colour in each special room
Plant-life of plenty with bright glossy blooms
Pixies and goblins with sweet fairy lights
My big peaceful Buddha so healing and bright
Amethyst, quartz and turquoise of blue
Poems of love and the things that are true
Cushions of silk with ribbons and beads
Flourishing thoughts of only to please
My family photos shine bright next to me
They fill my emotions with gladness and glee
A big wooded mirror, a magical ball
Pouches and potions hung high on my wall
A room for my healing and books for good health
They all sit on top of my practising shelf
Gold shiny singing bowls peaceful as bliss
Each room is filled with a magical wish
They fill me with joy and the promise of love
I now give my thanks to the dear Lord above

Treasures of the Heart

By Coral Dawn

<u>Love Is A Balanced Ocean</u>

Fear and anger do but dwell

They find a place inside your shell

They are not real, they cannot be

The egos' thoughts will mote it be

Loves the only thing that's real

It changes how we act and feel

Love can stay close by our side

Life is but an oceans tide

Treat yourself with love and grace

Your world will be a balanced place

Treasures of the Heart

By Coral Dawn

The Friend That Lives Inside Me

Deep inside my body is a friend I call my own
A friend that cares and loves me and a friend I've always known
She answers all my questions and she guides my sacred way
She sends me warming feelings so they'll keep my doubts at bay
She lives inside my senses and she kisses all my tears
She joins me through each special day
And leads me through the years
I get a feeling every time I need to make a choice
A tingle or a flutter or a softened, caring voice
I sometimes see a vision of a higher part of me
A happy, kind and gentle face with only love to see
She soothes me and she tells me that she loves me very much
She fills me up with wisdom and the dreams I sense and touch
I plead with her to heal me, and to mend my lonely heart
She tells me "trust in only love, your healing can then start"
I know of all she tells me is from wisdom I have learned
Until I live through only love my spirit will return

Treasures of the Heart

By Coral Dawn

The Tiny Waterfall

Up a windy road and on the right side of the hill
There is a tiny waterfall that's magical and real
It beckons you with wonder and it makes you want to stop
The sunlight glistens through the trees that rest upon the top
The sky above the bowing trees smiles down to you with love
The sounds of little birds at play surround you from above
The colours of the waterfall are such a sight to see
Shades of green with shiny glints that called to talk to me
Little flowers sprouting out to drink and quench their thirst
Tiny bubbles falling down and some about to burst
Next time that I pass this place the waterfall exists
I'll leave my blessings 'bove the tree, and all the hopes I wish

Treasures of the Heart

By Coral Dawn

The Field Of Sunflowers

Orange faces looking up and meeting with the sun
Yellow petals all around like feathers on each one
A track straight through the flower field, for folk to warm their hearts
With miles and miles of yellow-gold, each side the pathway starts
Softened petals dancing 'bout and laughing in the sky
Butterflies that settle 'pon their face before they fly
Some show hints of auric-gold, while edged with scarlet light
Lustrous as the setting sun before the dark of night
Seedy centres burnish-brown through lemon petal stars
Verdant leaves with golden glints, reflecting from afar
Bobbing 'bout like fairies in a field of magic wonder
Lucid as the sunlight of the days that promise longer
Bumble bees that mirror all the colours of each flower
Like shiny plates of honey in a landscape scented shower
Golden lives of happiness and joys that sway and sing
A warming sense of gratitude of every hopeful thing

Treasures of the Heart

By Coral Dawn

The Box At The Bottom Of The Stream

One day I sat beside the stream to soothe my tired mind
I brushed against the buttercups and prayed for dreams I'd find
Grasses touched me softly as they swept across my toes
I closed my eyes and prayed aloud for all my dreams to grow
I moved much closer to the stream and saw down to the ground
I found a box with golden bands and symbols all around
I stretched deep down to reach the box while pulling up my sleeve
Excitement swept upon my face for all I would retrieve
I got it out onto the ground and laid it on the grass
I wondered if this box would bring my dreams to life at last
I opened up the wooden lid to see what lie inside
I held the satin ribbons which my hopeful heart untied
Music played as light shone out to fill the summer breeze
A crystal sat inside the box with only thought to please
As clear as glass, a starry shape, with rainbows shining through
Willing me to place my dreams while watching as they grew
Magic happened on that day as rays of light emerged
All my dreams were listened to, their each and every word
I shut the box up tightly and I tied the ribbons too
I thanked the crystal with my love and all my heart now knew
I placed it back beneath the stream, while basking 'neath the sun
I prayed the box would help more folk, with all their dreams to come

Treasures of the Heart

By Coral Dawn

Thank You

Thank you is a phrase we say when grateful from the heart
It's felt with love and happiness and gladness plays a part
You may have done a deed of good; a prize you may have won
Gratitude for life itself can bring this feeling on
We give our thanks to God above for family and friends
For special homes we live in, for the love that never ends
A beautiful angelic voice, the summer sun so bright
A garden full of buttercups, the crescent moon at night
All these things and more deserve a thank you and a kiss
If we give them honestly the joy will not be missed

Treasures of the Heart

By Coral Dawn

The Hawk

Using wind to hold his wings he hovers in the sky
Scanning down to find his meal as sea-gulls pass him by
Rocks that live together offer welcome to the sea
Homing little creatures that the hawk can easily see
Sun that shines upon the waves like stars of midnight sky
As winds decrease their airy force the hawk begins to fly
Turquoise shapes the sun reflect upon the ocean tide
Frothy silken bubbles meet together at their side
He looks upon the ocean called St. Just without a doubt
Savouring the beauty and the magic inside out

Treasures of the Heart

By Coral Dawn

Thinking Of Our Love

Looking cross the ocean shore, thinking of our love
Wishing you were with me, as I shed a tear for you

Waves of warming glory and the love of all my dreams
Sandy kisses on my lips and all the love you bring
Come to me my darling, please embrace me in your arms
Bathe the sun of warming joy with hearts of soothing calm

Dreaming of your tender touch as ripples flow along
Your face indented in the sand, my feelings pulling strong
I look toward the rolling waves, I watch them hit the sand
I pray to God above me, "Will you help with all my plans"?

The sun looks down upon me as it warms my hopeful heart
I miss you my sweet darling, I'm so cold when we're apart
I trust in our tomorrow and the strength of love we hold
I dream of us together, and the meaning we behold

Two seagulls fly together, as I see the longing sign
I thank the Lord for when we meet with your heart touching mine

Treasures of the Heart

By Coral Dawn
The Robin

With face and chest of rusty-red
And white plump belly just been fed
With head of brown and wings to match
With long thin legs and soft-grey patch
A festive scene of sheer delight
A folk-lore choice, a joyful sight
His feathers dancing in the air
His song of beauty, sweet and fair
A warbled song from early dawn
Twiddle-eedee so soft and strong
He has a taste for sunflower hearts
His partial to some fruited tart
Grass-hoppers are his favourite treat
He finds a spot to rest and eat
Black feathers are his mating trait
He seeks to find his life-long mate
They softly stroke with bold display
They look toward their blessed day
They build their nest with moss and leaves
With grass and twigs and stems from trees
The female warms their eggs of blue
Her mate finds food the whole day through
When they hatch they stay close by
The parents answer every cry
Their song grows loud as Christmas nears
He voices thanks and whistling cheers
For all Gods' creatures wild and free
Display his love for all to see

Treasures of the Heart

By Coral Dawn

Angels

White and pure, a golden glow

Love and grace their hearts bestow

An infinite aura that glows with love

They heal and they guide us through heaven above

Our Guardian Angel stays close by our side

Our spiritual friend, our perpetual guide

Their feeling is light and a promise of truth

Their aura shines bright with such beauty and youth

Guidance they give and their deepest protection

They have sweet compassion and purest perfection

Their voices are gentle and consciously kind

They gift us with love that we seek hard to find

Sweetness and grace they will promise to bring

Their softness of words within each single thing

They'll always release any fear from our minds

By guiding our lives to the good that we find

For love is the answer to every desire

By striving for mercy our dreams will transpire

So when we show love and we ask for their touch

Our Angels will guide us and help us so much

Treasures of the Heart

By Coral Dawn

Colour

The blue night sky, the turquoise sea

The white summer-rose brings peace to me

The tall green grass, the yellow sun

The wood-brown trees for everyone

Autumn leaves, the purple pansy

The shepherd sky and the yellow tansy

The orange flame, the blue-birds song

Translucent rain and fierce, black storm

Reddened passion, magenta bright

Silver stars that shine with light

The cream-coloured house in fields of herbs

The trees of blossom and colours of words

The lavender lilac and iris of blue

They all bring joy in all they do

I close my eyes and think of love

I see warm sunshine from above

You'll see the colours deep inside

Oceans blue; the rolling tide

Give forth your thanks for joy to treasure

Then hold it in your hearts forever

Treasures of the Heart

By Coral Dawn

Gratitude

There's so many things to be grateful for
The changing tide and the beautiful shore
The kiss you are given from people you love
The sun that is shining from heaven above
The comforting touch when you feel you're in need
The food that has grown from a very small seed
The garden you enter to be close to God
The natural form of a nourishing pod
The grasses that dance with a warm summer breeze
The beautiful scene of a white forest freeze
The fields that surround us, the skies that are blue
They boost all our thank you's in all that we do
So when you feel troubled, unhappy and blue
Give and say thank you on each day that's new

Treasures of the Heart

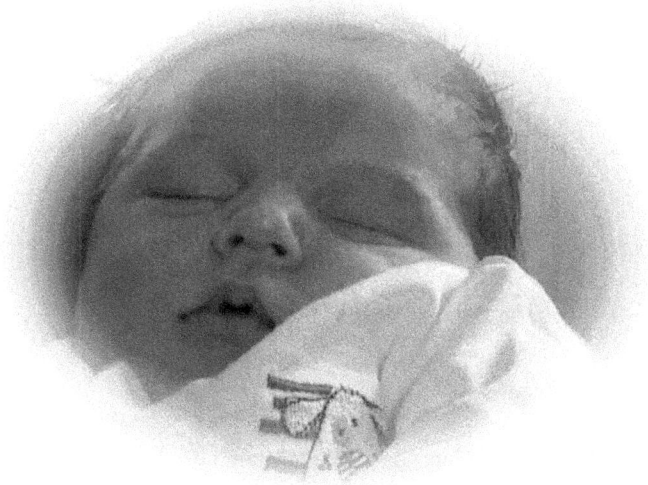

By Coral Dawn

Golden Sand

Misty sprays of golden sand

Dusty grains upon my hand

Covering soft upon my feet

Blowing through the summer heat

Yellow grains of powdered light

Bobbing through the sky so bright

Like a misty desert dune

Bright as sunshine light of noon

Dancing on the splashing waves

With honey hues of summer days

Softened dreams of gritty grains

Greeting wind across the plain

Settling up upon a cliff

Golden shapes of tender bliss

Chasing through the setting sun

Hints of scarlet in each one

Pictures in the twilight sky

Of dreams to catch as they go by

When I feel the golden sand

It rouses senses in my hand

It heals each flaw I hold inside

Each time I breathe the changing tide

Treasures of the Heart

By Coral Dawn

Hedgerows

Along the hedgerows wild and free, little eyes peep out at me
Finches, crests and sparrows too, feed below the sky of blue
Leafy litter on the ground; a beetle that a hedgehog found
Yellow trumpets looking through, with knapweed and its purple hue
Shelters made from dog-wood trees, gift their bowing canopies
Glossy leaves of creeping vines, catching sunlight as it shines
Voles and field mice scamper round
Finding seeds from dampened ground
Holly hedge and laurel too, hide the rabbit and the shrew
Yarrow with its snow-white face; Linnets chirping as they race
Toads go hopping through the trees; Maple blowing in the breeze
Basil with its heady smell; Foxglove with its crimson bell
Larger trees in hedging rows, is where the wrens and robins go
Hawthorn and the wild rose too, protect its wildlife all year through
There's life of plenty tearing round
Pleased with all the joy they've found
It's a beautiful sight of natural delight
Abundant in colour, wild and bright

Treasures of the Heart

By Coral Dawn

Live The Joy In Everything

Love's a sense of how you feel
It's always here, it's always real
An upset or some words of pain
A row you've had or doubts of blame
Love can win against it all
Its power can make you ten feet tall
You're child that speaks and makes you cry
Through all the love and ways you try
But love still lives inside your heart
A sense you feel in every part
I love you child do you not see
The love I hold inside of me
Do not dwell on worthless things
Live the joy in everything

Treasures of the Heart

By Coral Dawn

The Man That Sells Wood

His shop was small and full of wood
Chairs surrounding where he stood
He seemed a happy kind of man
A wise old soul who had a plan
He beckoned me to stay and laugh
His eyes showed me his knowing path
He made me smile with jokes he told
He seemed to have a heart of gold
His wooden things were sold with pride
His eyes lit up with every stride
Muddle everywhere I looked
With more in every little nook
His little shop shone out to me
With so much wood for all to see
This little man who spends his days
Selling wood to those who pay
If you meet this man of faith
You'll see such love upon his face
Much he knows, and tales he tells
Gifting others where he dwells

Treasures of the Heart

By Coral Dawn

Her Calling

As she walks, her ambience shows
She possesses an aura, a knowing glow
She remembers her gifts and lessons learned
She senses the reason for her return
Her life is serene yet ever learning
She feels others cries and heart-felt yearning
She programmes her crystals for followers' healing
Prayers of contentment she sends as she's kneeling
She trusts in the voice that she hears in her mind
To show her the answers she journeys to find
She places her hands on a young sickly child
She speaks with a voice that's so peaceful and mild
She hears asking cries from the wild-life and trees
Her pathway and visions want only to please
Her life is to aid folk as much as she can
It's why she is here, it's her spiritual plan
Her heart is unhappy of other folks sorrow
Her purpose is peace and the gracious tomorrow

Treasures of the Heart

By Coral Dawn

I Heard A Silent Lullaby

A quiet whisper came to me

To tell me how my life should be

I saw the pictures through the clouds

The voice I heard was soft and proud

Somewhere through the clouds up high -

I heard a silent lullaby

It told me of the love I hold -

And how my dreams would then unfold

Every day I'd check the sky to hear the silent lullaby

It always came with clouds of love

As I would search the sky above

Graceful wisps of dreamy sky

Shield the wisdom floating by

Answer when it beckons you

A peaceful sound so soft and true

The clouds now fill me up with words

Each of them I've clearly heard

They tell me always send your light

To brighten up the darkest night

If you're feeling sad and blue -

Look through clouds and listen too

All can hear the lullaby, if they really trust and try

Treasures of the Heart

By Coral Dawn

The Tree That Talks To Me

In a place called Respryn and beside a wooded lane
Exists a tree of wonder that I visit now and again
He's by a little river and he's bowing 'cross a seat
Waiting for the next time that we once again will meet
He stands so proud and sturdy with his branches reaching out
His many leaves of golden-green are dancing all about
He bears an air of energy, of life beyond compare
He calls to hold him tightly whilst he answers every prayer
I snuggle 'gainst him lovingly and merge my heart with his
I tell him all my worries, and of all that I can give
His arms reach down toward me
And his leaves brush 'gainst my face
He tells me that he loves me and he fills me up with grace
I pour some moonlight water down upon his thirsty roots
I spray a mist of sun-blessed rain, upon his tiny shoots
I hang a pouch of blessings for this place the tree exists
I thank the tree that talks to me, and answers every wish

Treasures of the Heart

By Coral Dawn

The Storm

I woke one day to crashing sounds of angry winter wind
It whirled on past and hit the trees and dared of more to bring
Sky as grey as darkened slate with clouds that drove along
Holding plants and sweeping leaves with breezes fast and strong
Dense and mighty crashing through the charcoal winter sky
Birds were fighting 'gainst the force as cold wind pushed them by
The rain fell down and soaked the ground in fast melodic time
The streams and rivers met as one and both became entwined
Thunder next, just like a drum that echoed through the air
Giving strong vibrations to the earth without a care
Lightening, bright and luminous, that lit up every cloud
Stirring through the raging sky that shone and crashed so loud
Branches moved both to and fro, obeying winter's call
Tumbling round in gusty wind then falling, one and all
Grasses swayed a murky dance of stormy winter stories
Every season lives in truth of all Gods' natural glory

Treasures of the Heart

By Coral Dawn

Waves Of Song

Waves of song that sing to me
Joyful love they bring to me
Miles of ocean cool and blue
Washing through the morning dew
Far upon a cliff top high
A cottage sits beneath the sky
It sits beneath the waves of song
In miles of ocean cool and strong
Breezes take the grains of sand
That gather on surrounding land
Showing glints of summer sun
That warms me of the songs to come
Waves that roll to find their way
Upon the shore of sunshine days
Seagulls join the oceans sound
Below the cottage that we found

Treasures of the Heart

By Coral Dawn

The Shop

Filled with crystals and healing gems
Coloured candles and books of poems
Beaded curtains and angel clocks
A glistening gift, a jewellery box
Fairies and pixies upon the shelf
Angel love and little elves
Healing cards and incense sticks
A box of promise, a crystal mix
A necklace display with love and meaning
An inspired sight and a gladdened feeling
The air is filled with magic inside
Every item is full of pride
Greetings cards are filled with joy
Wooded wands and children's toys
Everything chosen with special thought
A smile always added before it is bought
Rainbow crystals reflecting their beauty
Chimes and mobiles appealing dainty
The shop is so joyous for all to see
A special lady holds the key
It shows her soul and all her love
She always acts through God above
Abundance and wishes are graciously sent –
To this lady of kindness, with loving intent

Treasures of the Heart

By Coral Dawn

The Ghost Within My Mind

Foggy mist of scattered thoughts that keep my life in limbo
Willing to move forward but the bars lock tight the window
The ghost begins to chatter to the past I leave behind
The silvery mist of quandary that's the ghost within my mind

I like my life in order, everything within its place
Everything just flowing through in perfect time and space
Chaos doesn't suit my life of calmness and design
While silver mist engulfs me with the ghost that's in my mind

Whispers in my silent dreams that try to guide my way
I will the ghost to leave my mind and honour what I say
A steady beat of rhythm's what my heart can hope to find
And silver mist can dance upon the ghost within my mind

I follow plans of order, reaching out for hidden signs
Everything is moving on to simple happy times
While my life is peaceful I can hope its love I'll find
And when I do the mist will clear the ghost within my mind

Treasures of the Heart

By Coral Dawn

The Old Bench Of Wishes

Along a track of woodland and beside a flowing stream
A worn out bench of wishes has predicted every dream
Its wood is carved from sycamore that once was new as spring
With symbols edged around the seat of all that it could bring
Folk would sit upon the bench as years of thanks went past
They closed their eyes of wishes, and their dreams were true at last
The waters rippled softly and sweet flowers filled the breeze
As folk would visit through the years
The bench would always please
But now the seat is tired, it is worn and needs some care
Rest and love is needed to restore the wishing chair
It needs its symbols freshened and some polish on its seat
It needs the folk to give their love when next time they will meet
When it feels replenished and it gleams with love to see
She'll lure passers' to her side while resting 'neath a tree
They'll sit once more upon her and they'll wish for all they need
And as she fills them full of love, their hopes will all succeed

Treasures of the Heart

By Coral Dawn

Wind

Leaves are falling, autumn's calling
And wind whispers promise of more
It feels around the leaves and trees to show us what's in store
It finds its way to seaweed shore as gulls chase 'bout the sky
It dances 'pon the rippling waves and lifts the sand up high
It squeezes 'tween each tiny grain and throws it cross the shore
A pair of sea-gulls fight the force to let their spirits soar
It travels to a murky lake and reaches to its soul
It meets the waters' misty sprays, maintaining nature's role
It whisks through grass and shows its shapes rejoicing its direction
It blows the leaves of maple trees of auburn-gold perfection
The clouds grow dark and thickly dense and threaten of a gale
They clap against the darkened sky as rain soaks through the dale
Whistling tunes of windy songs as branches leave the trees
The waves grow huge and crash in time controlling mighty seas
As God reminds, we learn and grow to sense our sacred choice
Whilst mind controls the ego's prize
Love makes our hearts to rejoice

Treasures of the Heart

By Coral Dawn

The Summerhouse

I had a lovely summerhouse especially built for me
I'm dressing it with crystals and some pretty things to see
I'm going to use this summerhouse to write deep from my heart
I'll fill the house up with my love in every single part
It overlooks my garden filled with flowers, pots and herbs
With birds that sit upon the wall and whistle to my words
I'll add some dainty hanging chimes and fairies on the shelves
I'll even find a special place for all my little elves
Butterflies will greet me as I meet them at the door
Sage will sit outside the house, the left side on the floor
Scent of summer flowers will entrance the silent breeze
With tiny apples growing 'pon my many fruited trees
My cat called Esmerelda will be sitting by my feet
Looking up contented with her face so soft and sweet
I'm writing now to help some folk with healing and a prayer
Inside my house that sits upon my garden bright and fair

Treasures of the Heart

By Coral Dawn

Nature

The wind doth blow, the sun doth shine
The light reflects beyond all time
The roots reach deep inside the earth
Preparing life and giving birth
Leaves appear and flowers show
A beautiful picture a golden glow
It's just like life, ideas evolve
They grow and thrive, they take a hold
Then all at once they show their face
And then our hearts begin to race
The birth of nature and new ideas
Our lives become so very clear
For all new things that grow through love –
Will then ascend through God above

Treasures of the Heart

By Coral Dawn

The Mallard

A Mallard came to talk to me
A soft and gentle soul to see
He flapped his wings and blinked his eyes
I spoke to him to his surprise
He pecked the earth to find a worm
His beak was smooth, but very firm
He landed on the sunlit lake
As sunshine haze began to wake
He moved the water with his feet
I laughed at him upon my seat
He took a warming sunshine bath
Splashing water on the path
Showing off and bobbing round
Leaving puddles on the ground
I wonder if he'll know my name
If he meets me once again

Treasures of the Heart

By Coral Dawn

The Sky

One blissful, warming summers' day, the sky basked in the sunlight
The sun gave out its amber rays and bathed the day so bright
I saw a scene of mottled sky as flocks of crows cruised by
While taking in Gods' gift of love, they spread their wings to fly
The pureness of a single cloud showed softness and delight
A falcon soared so gracefully, he gained a soaring height
The growing breeze stretched with a sigh
And hummed a windy song
It blew the rays of sunlight, as it chased the air along
Showers of translucent rain were warm and softly falling
A glowing rainbow symphony then answered to its calling
It filled the sky with artistry and visions of Gods' grace
It arched above a jewelled lake, then journeyed into space
Crowds of pictures merged as one, uniting with the stars
Candescent as the crescent moon that glistened from afar
The story of our nature is a wonderful creation
We must make sure we treat it with our true appreciation
All things that are living are a gift we have to hold –
And if we act through kindliness, true joy we will behold

Treasures of the Heart

By Coral Dawn

Where I Go To Be With You

Cooling ripples on my toes that sink deep in the sand
Imprints at the ocean shore, of all our love and plans
Patterns of my longing thoughts in every sandy grain
All the hopes I want for us in every drop of rain

Salty sea that splashes me reminds me of our love
I dream that you are with me where I go to be with you

Shells of shiny colours calling, everywhere I go
I see your face reflecting on the waves that start to grow
We're singing songs I've written all along the rocky shore
Planning times together, that will light my heart once more

Waves that roll toward my heart remind me of our love
I dream that you are with me where I go to be with you

I see you smiling at me as I lay and close my eyes
You tell me that you love me, that my dreams won't tell me lies
The sun that shines above me, can remind me how we laugh
As silent sea engulfs me, in such softened peace at last

Sunny rays of happiness reminds me of our love
I dream that you are with me where I go to be with you

Treasures of the Heart

By Coral Dawn

Treasures Of The Heart

All my special poems are my treasures of the heart
Love is filled in every word and felt in every part
They all mean so much to me in so many different ways
They all having different meanings in the things they have to say
They fill my mind with pictures, like small stories of a dream
Where scenes and colours intermix, depending on the theme
My poetry flows from me and reflects the way I feel
I find it therapeutic and the words I write can heal
I hope to share with others all the love my poems hold
I hope that folk enjoy the many stories that I've told
I'm working on my next book based on fairy folk and elves
With a book of good intentions to improve us with good health
So I'll sit and write my poetry on each and every day
And put my heart within them all and everything I say

Treasures of the Heart

By Coral Dawn

Contributions to Treasures of the Heart (Special Edition)

Published, Edited and Created by Coral Dawn. All enquiries: -

www.coraldawn.com (The Coral Dawn site is under construction).

www.facebook.com/coral.dawn9026

coral.dawn222@gmail.com

Phone: - 01209 832140   Mobile: - 07876 491354

Production, Design, Layout and Publishing Facilitated by

Steve Evans.

All enquiries: - www.web-sites-plus.com

Steve@web-sites-plus.com

Phone: - 01202 873058   Mobile: - 07854 978913

Photography and Book Promotion by Gayle Force.

All enquiries: -

www.facebook.com/gayle.force1

Phone 01726 70786

All photographs are copyright Gayle Force© 2014

Treasures of the Heart

Family and friends that helped contribute to this book

My dearest Mother and Father. My Mother passed the gift of poetry to me, but more than that, both my Mother and Father were loving, sensitive, caring and very special souls. They taught me to be whom I am today, and to express myself through love and kindness. So because of their tenderness, their love as well as mine is inside every poem.

My special partner Rob has helped me in so many ways on my Treasures of the Heart journey. It's been emotional at times, but we have learnt a lot of things together along the way. I love him dearly with all of my heart.

My special brother Steve has helped me so much with this book. He has produced, designed and illustrated the book, and has been there twenty-four-seven for me. I am so grateful to him for the wonderful job he has done and for becoming a wonderful friend as well as my special brother.

Gayle Force. Gayle has become a good friend since our meeting in February and I would like to thank her for her lovely photography that I have added to this book to enhance each poems' story.

Gemma Coffey my very precious daughter, helped with suggestions for some of my favourite poems. We laughed and cried and became even closer than ever before.

Michelle and Jamie (my precious daughter and son). I would like to thank all of my children for their kind words of encouragement and their belief in me for the goals that I have set myself.

By Coral Dawn

Dawn Everett my very special cousin, listened, advised, but most of all she loved

Caroline Knight my very good friend, listened, encouraged and enjoyed our evenings of listening to my poetry.

Kim Williams my good friend helped me in many ways through my journey to where I am now in my life and because of that, she will always be special to me.

www.ingramcontent.com/pod-product-compliance
Lightning Source LLC
Chambersburg PA
CBHW071723090426
42738CB00009B/1863